Table of Contents

Introduction

Relapse prevention support groups are a new and innovative approach to recovery. The concept grew out of the desperate need of relapse-prone people to recover. Relapse support groups are self-help groups designed to support the growing number of recovering people who are using relapse prevention therapy as part of their recovery programs.

As more recovering people got involved in relapse prevention support groups, I began to get calls and letters asking for advice on how to start and maintain a group. These calls disturbed me because I didn't know how to answer the questions that I was being asked. So I began to do some research. I went right to the experts, the pioneers who have already started relapse prevention support groups and are learning how to make them work. I have attempted to combine what I have learned from numerous conversations across the United States and Canada and condense that information into a simple question-and-answer format. I have included the most commonly asked questions about relapse prevention and relapse prevention support groups. It is my goal to give you enough information to start a group if you want to do so.

This information comes from recovering people who have started relapse prevention support groups. Because these groups are so new, there are no *right* answers. Nothing is etched in granite. Some of the groups I've heard about succeeded. Others failed. I want to share with you my impressions of what helped the successful groups succeed and what caused the unsuccessful groups to fail. You will be given guidelines not absolute recommendations. Each group is unique, and those that succeed build upon the special strengths and weaknesses of their members. Successful groups focus heavily upon the needs of their members, give special attention to new members, keep the focus on identifying and managing warning signs, and allow for a diversity of discussion and feedback among members.

Now, on to the questions.

What Is Relapse?

Relapse is the process of becoming so dysfunctional in recovery that alcohol or drug use seems like a good idea. **Relapse warning signs** develop long before we begin to use alcohol or drugs. These warning signs are problems that lead to chemical use. They get out of control. One problem leads to another until we feel overwhelmed, confused, frustrated, and in unbearable pain.

Using alcohol or drugs is the last step in the process. It is rare to find someone who is "suddenly taken drunk." When people honestly examine the situations that led up to a relapse they almost always see a sequence of warning signs. We are usually unaware of what these warning signs are when they are happening. Why? No one has ever told us that warning signs exist, and even if we knew about them we have never learned how to manage them. As a result they attack when we least expect it. Many people who relapse have no real idea of what went wrong. They simply know that sobriety became so painful that they couldn't stand it and that alcohol or drug use seemed like a reasonable way to manage the pain.

The relapse process is often called building up to drink (BUD). There is a buildup of pain and problems that precede the relapse. We become so dysfunctional that we believe the only choices are to kill ourselves, collapse physically or emotionally, or self-medicate with alcohol or drugs.

Relapse prevention offers a fourth option. We can learn to recognize and manage the warning signs that are making us miserable in our sobriety.

Recovering people can have two types of relapse: a "wet relapse" in which they return to alcohol and drug use or a "dry relapse" in which they become dysfunctional without actually using alcohol or drugs. These dry relapses have been called dry drunks or white knuckle sobriety. They are dangerous for several reasons. First, they often cause us to return to alcohol and drug use. Second, they lower the quality of our sobriety and create unnecessary pain and problems. Finally, they can make us so miserable in sobriety that we collapse physically or emotionally or attempt suicide.

Dry relapses almost always precede wet relapses. Relapses, whether dry or wet, usually occur because we either fail to identify the warning signs that put us in risk of alcohol or drug use or we know what the warning signs are but don't do anything to cope with them while sober.

Knowing what our warning signs are is not enough. We must know what to do to manage those warning signs and be willing to do it. Relapse prevention is a program of action. We must be willing to do the leg work.

What Are the Common Warning Signs of Relapse?

People who relapse aren't suddenly taken drunk. Most of us experience warning signs that tell us we're in trouble. These warning signs can reactivate our denial and cause so much pain that self-medication with alcohol or drugs seems like a good idea. We don't consciously create these warning signs; they develop automatically. Most of us are not aware of them because we've never been trained to identify and manage them.

Warning signs are like fingerprints—we all have them but each one is different. Although most recovering people experience warning signs, each has a unique fingerprint. By looking at similarities we can learn from the experience of others and begin to deal with our own situation. Five steps usually precede chemical use.

First, we get **stuck in recovery**. We hit a problem or a part of the program that we are unwilling or unable to deal with.

Then we **deny the stuck point**. Instead of recognizing that we are stuck and asking for help, we lapse into denial and try to convince ourselves we're not really stuck. "Everything is OK," or so we tell ourselves.

Now we are ready to start **using other compulsions** to handle our pain. It hurts to be stuck in recovery, and the pain drives our stress levels up. We need to do something—anything—to manage the stress. Compulsive behaviors are great temporary stress reducers. The compulsion can be channelled into overwork, overeating, dieting, exercising, sexuality, relationships, religion, or shopping. It makes no difference which one we choose. The outcome is the same. We feel temporary relief, but the stress and pain come back. This is the problem with addictive behaviors: they make us feel good in the short run but weaken us in the long run.

Now we're vulnerable to the **trigger event**: something happens. It's not usually a big thing. It's something we could normally handle without getting upset. But this time something snaps inside. It feels like a trigger is pulled and something changes inside.

Our brain "checks out." Professionals call it **internal dysfunction**. We can't think clearly and our memory stops working. We swing between emotional overreaction and emotional numbness. We can't remember things. It's impossible to sleep restfully, and we get clumsy and start having accidents. Why? We're in so much pain that we can't function normally, and the trigger forced us to become aware of that pain.

When we can't function on the inside, it's only a matter of time until we're unable to function on the outside. This is called **external dysfunction**. We start making mistakes at work, creating problems with friends, families, and lovers, and neglecting our recovery programs.

Finally, as the problems grow one upon the other we start to **lose control**. Solving one problem creates two new ones to replace it. We start to feel like we are trying to hold three beach balls underwater at once. We get the first one down, then the second, but as we reach for the third, the first one pops back up again. It finally becomes obvious that we are out of control, and this frightens us. "I'm sober! I'm not drinking! Yet I'm out of control. If this is what sobriety is like, who needs it?"

The last step is using alcohol or drugs—the **relapse episode** itself. We're in so much pain that we come to believe we have only three choices: collapse physically or emotionally, commit suicide, or self-medicate with alcohol or drugs. Yes, you heard me right, *self-medicate!* Using alcohol or drugs as a medicine to make the pain go away starts to appear reasonable.

If we start to use alcohol or drugs, we feel ashamed and guilty. That causes us to use more alcohol and drugs which produces more guilt. We spiral out of control. Health and life problems are not far behind. If we don't get back into recovery we will eventually die.

Even if we don't use alcohol or drugs, we can still feel ashamed and guilty. We begin to think, "I'm sober but look how miserable I am—I must be defective or doing something wrong." Many of us try to stay sober by saying, "I'd rather be dead than drunk," and pretty soon we feel like killing ourselves. Many of us actually think about or attempt suicide. Others just hang in there until they have a stress collapse, develop a stress-related illness, or have a nervous breakdown. Still others use half measures to temporarily pull themselves together for a little while only to have the problems come back even more strongly later. This is partial recovery, and many people stay in it for years. They never get really well, but they never get drunk either.

What I have just described is called the relapse process and it's not rare. Most recovering people periodically experience some of these warning signs. About half can stop the process *before* they use chemicals or collapse. The other half revert to alcohol or chemical use, collapse, or kill themselves.

It's not a pretty picture. No wonder we don't want to think about relapse. It's depressing. The problem is that refusing to think about it doesn't stop it from happening. As a matter of fact, ignoring the early warning signs makes us more likely to relapse.

But there is hope. There is a method called **Relapse Prevention Planning** that can teach us to recognize early warning signs of relapse and stop them before we use alcohol and drugs or collapse.

What Is Relapse Prevention Therapy?

Relapse Prevention Therapy is the process of developing a comprehensive relapse prevention plan under the supervision of a Certified Relapse Prevention Specialist (CRPS). There are nine steps in developing the relapse prevention plan.

The first is **stabilization**. Relapse prevention planning probably won't work unless we are sober and in control of ourselves. This means we need to get detoxified and have at least a few good days of sobriety under our belts before we get started. We need to be able to think clearly, manage our feelings and emotions, and control our behavior in order to make relapse prevention planning work.

The second step is **assessment**. We need both a professional and a self-evaluation to accurately understand the problems that were caused by our past relapses. A few years ago it was difficult to find a relapse prevention specialist who could help us. Now there is a national listing with the CENAPS Corporation (18650 Dixie Highway, Homewood, IL 60430; phone 708/799-5000; FAX 708/799-5032). They'll send you a list for free if you provide a self-addressed stamped envelope.

The third step is relapse **education**. We need to learn about relapse, and it's not a bad idea to bring our family and Twelve Step sponsor with us. We need to know that there are warning signs that occur before we start using alcohol or drugs. And most importantly, we need to know that there is hope. We can recognize the early warning signs and stop them before it is too late.

The fourth step is **warning sign identification.** We need to identify the internal and external problems that lead us back to chemical use. Relapse can happen in one of two ways: (1) the warning signs can reactivate the denial of addiction by creating the mistaken belief we can safely use alcohol or drugs again, or (2) they can create so much pain and discomfort that we are tempted to use chemicals to self-medicate the pain.

There is seldom just one warning sign. Usually a series of warning signs build one upon the other to create relapse. It's the cumulative effect that wears us down. The final warning sign is simply the straw that breaks the camel's back. Unfortunately, many of us think it's the last warning sign that did it. As a result, we don't look for the earlier and more subtle warning signs that set the stage for the final disaster.

Each warning sign is a combination of two things—a problem and our reaction to the problem. Our reaction includes thoughts (we talk to ourselves about it), feelings (we develop body sensations and emotions), and actions (we do something about our thoughts and act out our feelings). In relapse prevention planning it's called our TFA. The "T" stands for *thinking,* the "F" stands for *feelings,* and the "A" stands for *actions* or behavior. Our TFA in response to a problem is usually more important than the problem itself because it can strengthen our recovery or weaken it by setting us up to relapse.

The goal of warning sign identification is to write

a list of personal warning signs that lead us from stable recovery back to chemical use. This list needs to identify the problems that lead to relapse and the irrational thoughts, unmanageable feelings, and self-defeating behaviors that emerge within us in response to the problems.

The fifth step of relapse prevention planning is **warning sign management.** Understanding warning signs is not enough. We need to learn how to manage them without resorting to alcohol or drug use. This means learning nonchemical problem-solving strategies that help us to identify high-risk situations and developing coping strategies. In this way we can diffuse our irrational thinking, manage our painful feelings, and stop the self-defeating behaviors before they lead to alcohol or drug use.

The sixth step is **recovery planning.** A recovery plan is a schedule of activities that puts us in regular contact with people who will help us avoid alcohol or drug use. We must stay sober by working the Twelve Step program and attending relapse prevention support groups that teach us to recognize and manage relapse warning signs. This is why I call relapse prevention planning a "Twelve Step Plus" approach to recovery.

The seventh step is **inventory training.** We must get in the habit of recognizing and managing warning signs by completing a morning inventory to plan our recovery activities and an evening inventory to review our progress and problems. This allows us to anticipate high-risk situations and monitor them for relapse warning signs. We need to take inventory work seriously because most warning signs are deeply entrenched habits that are hard to change. They return automatically when certain problems or stressful situations occur. If we aren't alert, we may not notice them until it is too late.

The eighth step is **family involvement**. A supportive family can make the difference between recovery and relapse. We need to encourage our family members to get involved in Alanon so they can recover from codependency. With this foundation of shared recovery, we can begin talking with our families about past relapses, the warning signs that led up to them, and how the relapse hurt the family. Most importantly, we can work together to avoid future relapse.

If we had heart disease we would want our families to be prepared for an emergency. Chemical dependency is a disease just like heart disease. Our families need to know about the early warning signs that lead to relapse. They must be prepared to take fast, decisive action if we return to chemical use. We can work out in advance—when we are in a sober state of mind—the steps they should take if we return to chemical use. Our very life could depend upon it.

The final step is **follow-up**. Our warning signs will change as we progress in recovery. Each stage of recovery has unique warning signs. Our ability to deal with the warning signs of one stage of recovery doesn't guarantee that we will recognize or know how to manage the warning signs of the next stage. Our relapse prevention plan needs to be updated regularly: monthly for the first three months, quarterly for the first two years, and annually thereafter.

How Are RP Support Groups Different from RP Therapy?

Relapse prevention support groups are self-help organizations. They are run by interested volunteers, not professional therapists, and they were originally designed to support individuals involved in relapse prevention therapy. The process of warning sign identification and management has been simplified to three steps for use in RP support groups. These are

1. *Warning Sign Identification:* the process of finding out the sequence of problems that caused relapse in the past and are likely to cause relapse in the future;

2. *Daily Inventory Work:* the process of consciously examining our daily actions in order to recognize the warning signs when they occur;

3. *Warning Sign Management:* the process of learning how to cope with relapse warning signs without having to use alcohol or drugs.

When Did the First Relapse Prevention Support Groups Begin?

The concept of relapse prevention is relatively new so the history of relapse prevention support groups is short. I first thought of starting relapse prevention self-help groups when I was doing relapse prevention therapy at Ingalls Hospital in Harvey, Illinois, in the early 1980s. Relapse prevention was offered as part of our regular treatment program, and our patients went to AA on a regular basis. As more people completed relapse prevention therapy they began having problems.

The concept of recognizing and managing relapse warning signs was a new and different approach to preventing relapse. Although the concept is consistent with AA and the Twelve Steps, the approach requires people to do things in recovery that are not, in a strict sense, Twelve Step work. As a result many people felt uncomfortable using AA and other Twelve Step meetings to work on warning sign identification and management.

We initially encouraged our patients to start AA groups for chronic relapsers. I got this idea from talking to AA members in Canada about "Golden Slippers Meetings." These were AA meetings attended by people who had tried to stay sober and couldn't do so in spite of regular AA attendance. Although I know of some relapse prevention AA meetings, most of the patients I worked with found it difficult to get them started.

Our next efforts were to encourage relapse-prone people to start separate meetings called relapse prevention support groups. These groups were started to allow people to work on warning sign identification and management while avoiding unnecessary controversy or conflict with the traditions of AA and other Twelve Step groups.

As far as I know the first successful relapse prevention support groups were organized in 1986 as a result of the efforts of Micki Thomas and the relapse prevention program at Father Martin's Ashley in Havre de Grace, Maryland. Ashley started a thirty-day relapse prevention therapy program in 1986 that taught patients how to identify and manage relapse warning signs. Most of the patients in the relapse prevention program came from out of state. After discharge the out-of-state patients had problems finding people they could talk with about identifying and managing their relapse warning signs. The Ashley staff began encouraging patients to start relapse prevention support groups.

About this time Merlene Miller and I published the book, *Staying Sober: A Guide for Relapse Prevention.* We included a chapter about starting relapse prevention support groups. As a result, a few relapse prevention support groups were born.

In the mid-1980s the concept of relapse prevention therapy became more popular. In 1986 the CENAPS Corporation began the first National Certification Program for Relapse Prevention Specialists. These certified specialists encouraged their patients to start relapse support groups. Many treatment centers began relapse prevention programs. They also encouraged their patients to start relapse prevention support groups.

Many patients who have completed relapse prevention therapy have attempted to start relapse prevention support groups but there were and continue to be problems. The biggest problem is that nobody really knows how to run relapse prevention support groups because they are so new. We're still experimenting and learning by trial and error.

In 1988 we decided to collect information about the relapse prevention support groups that were operating to find out what makes them work. We now have a directory of relapse prevention support groups kept by the CENAPS Corporation. The list is small but growing. You can get a copy of it by sending a self-addressed stamped envelope to Relapse Prevention Support Groups, The CENAPS Corporation, 18650 Dixie Highway, Homewood, Illinois 60430, or call 708/799-5000. If you know of any relapse prevention support groups that are not on the list, please encourage them to contact us and get listed.

What Are the Basic Principles upon Which Relapse Prevention Support Groups Are Built?

Relapse prevention support groups are based on two basic principles: (1) there are predictable warning signs that precede relapse; (2) relapse can be prevented if people learn how to recognize and responsibly manage those early warning signs.

These principles translate into three major goals. The first goal is to identify the early warning signs that lead to relapse. The second goal is to learn how to recognize the warning signs as they occur in our sobriety. The third goal is to learn how to manage those warning signs without having to use alcohol or drugs.

Goals of Relapse Prevention Support Groups:
1. Identify relapse warning signs
2. Learn how to recognize the warning signs as they occur
3. Learn how to manage the warning signs without having to use alcohol or other drugs

---

These principles and major goals are important because they give the groups a special purpose or function. It seems that the groups which keep their focus upon identifying and managing relapse warning signs tend to succeed. Those that lose this focus tend to fail.

What Are the Membership Requirements of a Relapse Prevention Support Group?

The only requirements for membership are (1) a recognition that we are alcoholic or chemically dependent and must abstain from all mood-altering drugs (including alcohol) in order to recover and (2) a desire not to relapse.

Although relapse prevention support groups are primarily designed for people who have had one or more wet relapses in the past, we find that it is best to allow anyone who wants to avoid relapse to join. It is better to be inclusive rather than exclusive. It is also better to help people avoid their first relapse than to insist that they get drunk in order to learn how *not* to get drunk.

How Are Relapse Prevention Support Groups Related to Alcoholics Anonymous (AA) and Other Twelve Step Programs?

Relapse prevention support groups are not AA meetings nor are they Twelve Step meetings. Relapse prevention support groups have special formats designed to help members identify and learn how to manage relapse warning signs. Most of us consider relapse prevention support groups to be an adjunct to and *NOT* a replacement for AA and other Twelve Step meetings. Relapse prevention group members are strongly encouraged—but not required—to attend Twelve Step meetings and actively work the Twelve Steps.

Most relapse prevention support groups have decided that it is best to remain separate from but cooperative with Twelve Step programs. By keeping the goals and purposes of relapse prevention support groups separate from the goals and purposes of AA, confusion and conflicts can be avoided.

Is There a Standard Format for Relapse Prevention Support Group Meetings?

Although the exact format for meetings will vary from group to group, there is a standard agenda that many groups have found helpful to use as a starting point. It includes the following:

An Opening Statement: Most meetings start with the chairperson announcing the name of the meeting, introducing himself or herself, and welcoming the people who are attending, especially the newcomers who are there for the first time. Most groups develop an introductory statement that includes the purpose of the relapse prevention support group and explains that it is cooperative with but not affiliated with AA and other Twelve Step programs.

A Quiet Time: The chairperson then asks for a brief period of silence to allow people to relax, clear their minds, and prepare themselves to benefit from the meeting.

The Lead Presentation: The chairperson asks someone to give a lead presentation. This person is invited in advance to speak so he or she has time to prepare. This lead presentation can consist of the reading of topic material such as the ''Phases and Warning Signs of Relapse'' or the telling of his or her recovery and relapse story which describes specific warning signs and how he or she is managing them.

Break: A brief break is announced. The refreshments served during the breaks should be decaffeinated beverages and *not* consist of sweets or refined carbohydrates. Snacks such as peanuts, fruits, and cheeses are appropriate. Caffeine and sugars can create adverse mood states that can trigger relapse warning signs.

Comments: Each member will have a chance to comment briefly on the lead presentation. It is the responsibility of the chairperson to assure that all members have a chance to comment. Each comment should be no longer than two to three minutes. When one person comments, it is the responsibility of the other group members to listen. There seems to be an 80/20 rule: 80 percent of what we learn comes from listening to others; 20 percent of what we learn comes from making comments. If we want to learn how to prevent relapse, we need to learn how to listen to and understand others so we can learn to understand ourselves.

Questioning, confrontation, and feedback are not allowed during the commenting section of the meeting. The goal of comments is for everyone to be given the opportunity to talk in a safe environment where they will not be criticized, confronted, or questioned. It has been our experience that if a new member feels that he or she is listened to, understood, taken seriously, and affirmed, *they will come back.* If they are questioned, challenged, and confronted, *they often will not.* The comment period is designed to create an atmosphere that is safe, supportive, and honest.

The Feedback Session: The final segment of the meeting is generally a feedback session. It is designed for individuals who want to present their own warning signs and management strategies and receive feedback from other group members. The individual briefly presents the warning sign he or she is dealing with. The group then has an opportunity to ask clarifying questions and give feedback. This is done in a structured manner. First, group members are encouraged to ask questions about anything they did not understand about the warning sign or how the person is attempting to manage it. After that each member is given the opportunity to give feedback to the person who presented a warning sign.

Good feedback covers four concerns:
1. What I think your warning sign is and how I see that you are managing it.
2. How I felt about you while you were talking and responding to questions.
3. The strengths I see that you have that will help you to manage these warning signs.
4. The weaknesses I see that may prevent you from managing the warning signs.

The feedback session needs to be voluntary. No one should be forced or coerced to present issues and receive feedback. It is also important that people giving feedback learn how to do so in a way that is rigorously honest but yet loving and supportive at the same time. The goal is to support the group members while pointing out problems that may cause future relapse. Harsh confrontation, name calling, insults, or angry outbursts are never appropriate during the feedback session. The chairperson or other group members need to stop such behavior should it occur.

Adjournment: Most meetings are either one-and-a-half or two hours long. If the meeting has a lead, comments, and a feedback session, it generally takes a full two hours to get through the agenda.

Are There Different Types of Meetings?

Yes. As we experiment with different ways of running the meetings, major types of meetings have emerged. These are:

1. warning sign meetings,
2. speaker meetings,
3. cross-talk or discussion meetings.

Let's look briefly at each type of meeting.

Warning Sign Meetings: During warning sign meetings, the members read aloud and discuss the warning signs that precede relapse. A typical meeting is conducted as follows: The group spends about ten minutes reading from *The Phases and Warning Signs of Relapse.* (This pamphlet is available from Herald House/Independence Press, P.O. Box HH, Independence, MO 64055, 1-800-767-8181. The warning signs are also printed in the books, *Staying Sober: A Guide for Relapse Prevention* and *The Staying Sober Workbook.*)

Group members then discuss their personal reactions to the warning signs that were read. The key focus of warning sign meetings needs to be on the personal reactions of the members to what is read. The group is designed to be a safe place where members can talk about relapse warning signs and how to manage them. Each member is encouraged to comment about his or her thoughts (how we think these warning signs apply to us), feelings (our emotional reactions to thinking about and talking about our warning signs), and actions (the behaviors we need to change in order to manage those warning signs). We have come to recognize that warning sign management requires that we change our thinking, feelings, and actions. To help us remember these three levels of change, many of us use the initials **TFA** to help keep us focused.

Many relapse prevention support groups have failed or nearly failed because they placed their primary focus on reading materials at meetings rather than on helping members understand the basic concepts of relapse prevention and changing the thoughts, feelings, and actions that lead to relapse. It is generally unwise to read any literature for longer than ten minutes in any meeting. The life and energy of the meeting is dependent upon sharing experiences, strength, and hope with one another. When the readings are too long, many members get bored or disillusioned and stop coming.

Speaker Meetings: The second type of meetings are speaker meetings. At a speaker meeting one of the members is asked to prepare a talk. The talk can focus on a single warning sign that he or she experienced and what was done to manage that warning sign. Or the person can focus on telling the story of past relapse and recovery history, highlighting the major warning signs that led to relapse and how the person learned to manage those warning signs sober.

A good relapse prevention talk that focuses on a single warning sign will answer the following questions:

1. What is the specific warning sign that I am going to talk about?

2. How did this warning sign cause me to use or want to use alcohol or drugs in the past?

3. How did I identify the warning sign as an important problem?

4. What did I do to manage the warning sign and stay sober?

5. What worked and what didn't work?

A good relapse prevention talk that tells the story of our relapse history will answer the following questions:

1. When was my first serious attempt at sobriety, how long did I stay sober, and what relapse warning signs caused me to return to alcohol or drug use?

2. How many relapse episodes have I had (both wet and dry)?

3. What warning signs occurred during each period of sobriety?

4. What have I learned to do to manage those warning signs?

5. What are the current warning signs that I need to be alert for and what am I doing to recognize and manage them?

It is important for new members to set the goal of giving a talk at a meeting. The first talk new members give typically focuses on discussing the most critical warning sign that has led to relapse in the past. After they have thoroughly reviewed and learned from their past relapse history, they can then tell their entire story, what they learned from it, and what they are now doing differently that is helping them identify and manage relapse warning signs.

Cross-talk or discussion meetings: The third type of meetings are cross-talk or discussion meetings. The goal of these meetings is for members to share ideas with one another about a selected topic. The group leader selects the topic for the evening and gives a brief lead presentation that introduces key ideas about that topic. The leader then guides a discussion of members' reaction to the topic.

The general questions that the leader will use to encourage discussion are:

1. What are your thoughts about tonight's topic?

2. What feelings do you have about tonight's topic?

3. What areas of agreement do you have with what has been said so far?

4. What areas of disagreement do you have with what has been said so far?

5. What is the most important thing you have learned from this discussion?

6. What are you going to do differently as a result of what you have learned?

It is important for the leader to give all members an opportunity to comment.

What Is a Relapse Prevention Sponsor? Why Is It Important to Have One?

A relapse prevention sponsor is someone who regularly attends relapse prevention support groups and who has developed a written relapse prevention plan for himself or herself. Sponsorship is critical. Every member of a relapse prevention support group is strongly encouraged to have a relapse prevention sponsor *and* to sponsor someone.

Relapse prevention support groups are new, and we are just beginning to experiment with sponsorship as a key activity in relapse prevention. Many relapse prevention sponsors have reported that it is helpful to guide the person they are sponsoring through a series of activities or exercises. The exercises that are most often used are as follows:

Exercise 1: Reviewing the most recent relapse. The sponsor discusses with the new member his or her most recent relapse and the period of sobriety that preceded it. The major focus is to help the new member reconstruct the exact sequence of thoughts, feelings, actions, and events that occurred while sober that caused a return to alcohol or drug use. The sponsor asks the new member to tell the story of the most recent relapse in a private conversation, write it down, and tell it in the relapse prevention support group.

It is important for new members to talk about their most recent relapse privately with a sponsor before they tell their story at a meeting. Talking about this story can be painful and frightening.

Many members prefer to tell the story of their most recent relapse in bits and pieces when they comment at meetings before they feel comfortable telling the whole story at a speakers meeting.

Exercise 2: Reconstructing the alcohol and drug-use history. The sponsor helps the new member to develop a written alcohol and drug-use history. The goal is to help the person to understand that he or she is chemically dependent and cannot control alcohol and drug use. Relapse prevention is designed for people who already know they are addicted, must abstain from alcohol and other drugs, and need to work a recovery program. If they don't believe these three things they would probably be better off going to AA meetings than attending relapse prevention support groups. Relapse prevention works best with people who have tried to use a recovery program in the past but have failed to stay sober. It is an additional tool not a replacement for basic recovery planning. The alcohol and drug-use history will help new members to determine their level of recognition and acceptance of their disease.

Exercise 3: Recovery and relapse history. The sponsor helps the new member develop a written recovery and relapse history. Putting it all down on paper may seem like a lot of work, but this is an essential step in coming to grips with the problem.

Exercise 4: Reading and discussing the warning sign list. During a private conversation, the relapse sponsor asks the new member to read the warning sign list out loud and to stop at warning signs he or she doesn't understand, can't identify with, or that stir up strong memories or emotions. New members often become frightened and depressed or have difficulty understanding and remembering the warning signs. By reading the warning signs out loud with a sponsor they are better able to understand and remember the warning signs and deal with the shame, guilt, and pain that is stirred up by reading them. Most sponsors report that they learn something new about themselves every time they read the warning signs through with a new member.

Exercise 5: Developing a personal warning sign list. The sponsor works with the new member to develop a written list of personal warning signs. This is the most important step. If relapse prevention is to succeed we must have a written list of relapse warning signs. Without a personal warning sign list we won't know what caused us to use alcohol or drugs in the past and we won't be able to learn how to manage those warning signs more effectively in the future. To develop a personal warning sign list new members are asked to:

a. select five warning signs from the master warning sign list that they identify with;

b. describe a specific past experience with each of these five warning signs and discuss these past experiences in detail with their sponsor and at the relapse prevention support group meetings;

c. discuss how each of these five warning signs may affect their recovery in the future;

d. write a final warning sign list that captures the general sequence of events that leads from stable recovery to relapse; and

e. read the list at a meeting and explain how they developed it.

Each warning sign on the list should contain a summary title, a description, and the typical thoughts, feelings, and actions (TFAs) related to that warning sign.

The summary title is a word or short phrase that captures the meaning of the warning sign. I'll use the example of one person named Fred who listed "Isolation" as a summary title.

A description is a short paragraph that describes what happens when we experience the warning sign. Fred described his isolation in this way: "I know I am in trouble with my recovery when I stop talking to others, stay home, and avoid people that I know."

Next comes a description of the typical thoughts we think when experiencing the warning sign. Fred wrote, "When I isolate I tend to think there is something wrong with me and nobody cares."

After that we describe the feelings we have when we experience the warning sign. Fred wrote, "When I isolate myself I usually feel depressed, angry with myself for being so antisocial, and angry with others for not caring."

Finally we write a description of our actions—what we do—when we are experiencing the warning sign. Fred wrote, "When I isolate I come late to meetings, sit quietly by myself, don't talk with anyone, make minimal comments, and leave early."

Exercise 6: Developing management strategies. The sponsor helps the new member select a critical warning sign and develop strategies for managing it without using alcohol or drugs. The critical warning is one that places the person in risk of relapse within the next four to six weeks. The management strategy itself contains methods for coping with the warning sign.

Warning signs can be managed on a number of levels. When managing a warning sign on the **situational level** we avoid situations that trigger the warning sign. When managing at the **behavioral level** we change what we do when the warning sign is activated. Instead of blindly repeating self-defeating behaviors that make the warning sign worse, we try something different. We do something that will turn the warning sign off. When managing at the **thinking level** we interrupt the addictive thinking that is activated by the warning sign. When managing at the **feeling level** we identify, talk about, and responsibly manage the uncomfortable feelings that are triggered by the warning sign.

The biggest challenge in relapse prevention is to begin managing warning signs at the **belief level** by changing our view of ourselves, other people, and the world that cause us to react to these warning signs in self-destructive ways. This fundamental change in belief is often described as the spiritual level of relapse prevention.

Exercise 7: Discussing problems and pro-
gress. The sponsor is available to discuss progress
and problems the new member is having in identifying and managing relapse warning signs. The
sponsor also encourages the new member to attend relapse prevention support group meetings
regularly and discuss his or her progress and problems.

Exercise 8: Telling your recovery and relapse
story. Once new members have developed a
period of stable recovery, reconstructed their
history, developed a warning sign list and management strategies, they are ready to tell their story at
a meeting. This process of getting ready to tell their
story should take from four to six weeks. If they
wait too long to get it done, they might get drunk
before the process has a chance to work.

Relapse prevention therapy works best if the ef-
fort is put in up front. This is the best way to over-
come the fear, shame, and guilt associated with
relapse. Roll up your sleeves and get involved.
Start talking at meetings, get a sponsor, complete
the relapse prevention exercises to the best of your
ability, and tell your story.

Don't try to be perfect. Keep it simple and do the
best you can. No one ever does a great job the first
time around. Relapse prevention means a willingness to inventory ourselves constantly and find
new ways of understanding and managing our relapse warning signs.

How Is Sponsorship Different from Counseling or Therapy?

There are several major differences between being a sponsor and being a counselor. Sponsors are not professionals and do not have professional training. As a result they simply help another person build a relapse prevention play by completing a series of exercises. The sponsor does not interpret, judge, or give advice. The sponsor explains what relapse warning signs are and how they can be managed. The sponsor shares personal experience with the relapse prevention process and encourages the new members to give it a try.

The sponsor is there to support and encourage the new member in identifying and learning how to manage relapse warning signs. If problems come up—and they usually do—that the sponsor doesn't know how to handle, the new member should be encouraged to go into counseling with a Certified Relapse Prevention Specialist.

Counselors who are certified in relapse prevention therapy have learned how to use powerful therapy procedures in conjunction with the basic relapse prevention exercises to identify warning signs and teach management skills. They are also trained in helping people recover from related psychological or relationship problems that often contribute to relapse.

A common mistake is that a relapse prevention sponsor tries to assume too much responsibility for the person he or she is sponsoring. *Remember, it is not your job to keep anyone sober but yourself.*

Easy does it. You don't help anyone by trying to control them. Select who you sponsor carefully. If they are not willing to work at writing down their history, warning signs, and management strategies, they may not be motivated to avoid relapse. Talk with them about it and refuse to keep sponsoring them unless they start investing some time and energy in making the process work. If sponsorship ever threatens your own sobriety, stop sponsoring. Don't be a sponsor *to* someone else unless you have a sponsor *for* yourself.

When Is Relapse Prevention Finished?

Relapse prevention is a process. It is a program of action. As such it is never really complete, but the process does keep getting easier and more effective. As we learn more about ourselves and our warning signs, we become skilled in doing inventory work and recognizing the warning signs when they occur. We develop effective skills for managing the warning signs before they spiral out of control.

We have a disease called alcoholism not "alcohol-*wasm*." The disease doesn't go away; it just goes into remission. Anytime we experience stress, the relapse warning signs (the sobriety-based symptoms of our disease) can return. This is neither good nor bad. It is simply the reality of our disease. If we want to stay in recovery, we must learn to recognize and manage those warning signs while sober.

A Final Word

Knowledge alone is not enough. We must put the knowledge into action. I hope the information about relapse prevention support groups that we have discussed is helpful to you. I learned most of these ideas and methods from relapse-prone people who were struggling to stay sober. If you attempt to use anything you heard here or develop some new ideas and approaches, please keep me informed. Remember, our main goal is to help chemically dependent people stay sober by identifying the early warning signs of relapse and learning how to manage them without using alcohol or other drugs. I truly believe that there is no such thing as a hopeless alcoholic; there are simply alcoholics who haven't yet learned about relapse prevention.

Appendixes

Appendix 1

Preamble Read at the Start of RP Support Group Meetings

Relapse prevention support groups are structured meetings designed to help relapse-prone persons and others concerned about the possibility of relapse. The only requirements for membership are a recognition that we are chemically dependent and a desire not to relapse.

The purpose of the group is to help us recognize the personal warning signs that lead to relapse and to learn how to manage them effectively without using alcohol or other drugs. The relapse prevention support group is not designed as a substitute for AA or professional counseling. Members are encouraged—but not required—to attend AA or other Twelve Step meetings regularly and to seek professional counseling and therapy.

The major factors that make the relapse prevention support group effective are

1. the development of a written list of personal relapse warning signs;

2. the completion of daily inventories to identify warning signs early;

3. the development of warning sign management strategies that can be used to stop the warning signs before they get out of control;

4. the willingness to talk openly and honestly about our warning signs and what we are doing to identify and manage them; and

5. the willingness to listen to the comments and

feedback of other group members.

As a participant in the relapse prevention support group, we are encouraged to prepare for meetings by writing and continually updating a written list of personal relapse warning signs and the methods we can use to manage them while sober. We also are encouraged to discuss any thoughts, feelings, or behaviors that we believe may put us in risk of relapse.

Many of us find that having a relapse prevention sponsor is necessary in developing and updating our relapse prevention plan. We also find that by sponsoring others we develop better skills at recognizing and managing our own warning signs.

There are no hopeless, chemically dependent people. Recovery is possible even for persons with long histories of chronic failure at recovery. The key to recovery is a combination of professional treatment, self-help group involvement based on the Twelve Steps of AA, and participation in a relapse prevention support group.

Appendix 2
Standard Meeting Agenda

An Opening Statement: Welcome to the _____ night meeting of the relapse prevention support group. My name is (*introduce self by first name and last initial*). I would like to extend a special welcome to anyone who is here for the first time. Would you please raise your hand and introduce yourself by your first name only.

I want to assure the newcomers that there is hope. If you want, one of the established members will meet with you after the meeting to explain how the group operates.

A Quiet Time: I would like to begin this meeting with a quiet time. Take a deep breath, relax, and clear your minds. In this moment of silence reflect upon what you need to discuss tonight in order to stay sober.

The Preamble: Before the meeting I asked (*name the person who will be reading the preamble*) to read our preamble. Would you please do that now?

The Lead Presentation: The lead presentation tonight will be (*introduce the speaker, define the topic, or identify the material that will be read*). (Keep the lead presentation to thirty minutes or less.)

Break: We will now take a brief break. Please notice that our beverages are decaffeinated and that we do not serve sweets or refined carbohydrates. This is because many recovering persons have found that caffeine and sugars can create adverse mood states that can trigger relapse warning signs. If you choose to smoke, please do so outside the meeting room.

Comments: Let's now reconvene. During this portion of the meeting we have an opportunity to comment briefly on the lead presentation. To assure that all of us have a chance to comment, I ask that no one speak for longer than two to three minutes. (If the group is larger than twenty persons, split into smaller discussion groups of about ten persons each. Try to assure that there are at least several established members in each of the groups.)

It has been our experience that many of us have difficulty listening to others. If we want to learn how to prevent relapse, we need to learn how to listen to and understand the problems of others. In this way we can learn to understand ourselves.

Our goal is to create a safe environment where we can talk without the fear of being criticized or confronted. As a result, questioning, confrontation, and feedback are not allowed during the commenting section of the meeting. If you would like feedback on specific problems, there will be a feedback session immediately following the comments. Who would like to begin the comments?

The Feedback Session: During this segment of the meeting individuals will have the opportunity to present their own warning signs and management strategies and receive feedback from other group members. Participation is strictly voluntary. The procedure goes like this: First one person presents the warning sign he or she is dealing with. The group then has an opportunity to ask clarifying questions and give feedback.

In giving feedback, please be honest but loving and supportive at the same time. Harsh confrontation, name calling, insults, or angry outbursts are not appropriate and will not be tolerated.

Adjournment: Thank you for coming. Our next meeting will be held (*identify the time, day, and place*). Would you all please stand and join me in the Relapse Prevention Pledge:

No matter how bad things get, I will not use alcohol or drugs today. I know that alcohol and drug use is not a solution. Chemical use will only make my problems worse! I pledge to work at identifying the warning signs that set me up to relapse. I pledge to develop positive ways for coping with those warning signs while sober. I pledge to complete a daily inventory of my progress and problems.

Appendix 3

The Relapse Prevention Pledge

No matter how bad things get, I will not use alcohol or drugs today. I know that alcohol and drug use is not a solution. Chemical use will only make my problems worse! I pledge to work at identifying the warning signs that set me up to relapse. I pledge to develop positive ways for coping with those warning signs while sober. I pledge to complete a daily inventory of my progress and problems.

Appendix 4

Writing a Personal Warning Sign List

If relapse prevention is to succeed we must have a written list of relapse warning signs. Without one we won't know what caused us to use alcohol or drugs in the past and won't be able to learn how to manage those warning signs more effectively in the future.

To develop a personal warning sign list new members are asked to:

1. select five warning signs from the master warning sign list that you identify with (see the pamphlet, *The Phases and Warning Signs of Relapse,* or the books, *Staying Sober: A Guide for Relapse Prevention* and *The Staying Sober Workbook,* which are available from Herald House/Independence Press, P.O. Box HH, Independence, MO 64055; 1-800-767-8181 or 800-252-5010;

2. describe a specific past experience with each of these five warning signs and discuss these past experiences in detail with your sponsor and at the relapse prevention support group meetings;

3. discuss how each of these five warning signs may affect your recovery in the future;

4. write a final warning sign list that captures the general sequence of events that leads from stable recovery to relapse. Each warning sign on the list should contain a summary title, a description of the warning sign, and the typical thoughts, feelings, and actions (TFAs) related to that warning sign;

5. read the list at a meeting and explain how you developed it and what you learned about yourself by writing it.

Here is an example of how to write a warning sign:

Summary Title: Isolation

Description: "I know I am in trouble with my recovery when I stop talking to others, stay home, and avoid people that I know."

Thoughts: When I experience this warning sign I tend to think there is something wrong with me and nobody really cares.

Feelings: When I experience this warning sign I usually feel depressed, angry with myself for being so antisocial, and angry with others for not caring.

Actions: When I isolate I come late to meetings, sit quietly by myself, don't talk with anyone, make minimal comments and leave early."

Appendix 5

Guidelines for Telling Your Story

There are two types of relapse prevention talks.

The first type of talk focuses on a single warning sign and will answer the following questions:

1. What is the specific warning sign that I am going to talk about?

2. How did this warning sign cause me to use or want to use alcohol or drugs in the past?

3. How did I identify the warning sign as an important problem?

4. What did I do to manage the warning sign and stay sober?

5. What worked and what didn't work?

The second type of relapse prevention talk that tells the story of our relapse history will answer the following questions:

1. When was my first serious attempt at sobriety, how long did I stay sober, and what relapse warning signs caused me to return to alcohol or drug use?

2. How many relapse episodes have I had (both wet and dry)?

3. What warning signs occurred during each period of sobriety?

4. What have I learned to do to manage those warning signs?

5. What are the current warning signs that I need to be alert for and what am I doing to recognize and manage them?

The resources shown on the following pages are designed for use directly with relapse-prone people. The powerful videotapes teach relapse prevention skills.

**STAYING
SOBER
A Guide
for Relapse
Prevention**

by Terence T. Gorski and Merlene Miller

Staying Sober explains practical methods for understanding and preventing relapse. This book was designed to meet the needs of persons recovering from chemical dependence. It presents easy-to-understand information about chemical dependence, the warning signs that precede relapse episodes, and methods for recognizing and managing relapse warning signs.

This book is designed as a recovery manual for persons seriously concerned about preventing relapse. The information is especially useful for

- recovering people with a history of relapse.
- people with long-term sobriety who want to be sure they have covered all the bases in preventing relapse.
- spouses of recovering chemically dependent people who desire more information about relapse.
- counselors looking for an effective manual for teaching patients about relapse and relapse prevention.

To Order, Call Toll-Free 1-800-767-8181

STAYING SOBER WORKBOOKS
Exercise Manual and Instruction Manual
by Terence T. Gorski

Staying Sober Workbooks are comprised of the Exercise Manual and the Instruction Manual. The books are designed to be used along with Staying Sober: A Guide for Relapse Prevention by Terence T. Gorski and Merlene Miller. The step-by-step approach used in the workbooks will be most helpful to persons in individual or group counseling sessions who are recovering from chemical dependency.

Readers will be guided in examining the entire relapse process to better understand why they relapse and how they can prevent relapse from occurring. This method has been proven successful among many recovering alcoholics and those with chemical dependencies. These proven principles of relapse prevention planning, based on the CENAPS model of treatment, are presented in an understandable, workable way.

MISTAKEN BELIEFS ABOUT RELAPSE
by Terence T. Gorski
and Merlene Miller

Many addicts relapse because they don't know the facts. They accept ideas about relapse that just aren't true.

This booklet describes the most common misconceptions about relapse and explains the dangers of accepting and living by them. It can be read quickly and easily and is a valuable aid for helping you or someone you care about prevent relapse.

THE PHASES AND WARNING SIGNS OF RELAPSE
by Terence T. Gorski and Merlene Miller

This pamphlet contains a complete description of the ten phases and the thirty-seven warning signs of relapse that form the basis of the *CENAPS Model of Relapse Prevention Planning.*

The original thirty-seven warning signs have been rewritten to be more easily understood. It includes the results of recent clinical studies that indicate alcoholics may experience problems other than alcohol/drug use as a result of this syndrome.

THE RELAPSE DYNAMIC (The Original Thirty-seven Warning Signs)
by Terence T. Gorski

The Relapse Dynamic is a brief and inexpensive three-fold flyer that contains the original 1973 version of the thirty-seven warning signs of relapse.

This brochure has been used for over ten years as a guide to relapse warning sign identification. The one-page format and volume prices make it ideal for use with community and patient education programs.

"**Triad** by Cynthia Downing makes a major contribution to understanding the emerging models of chemical dependence treatment. Her comparison of AA, the Minnesota Model, and the CENAPS is superb!"

Terence T. Gorski

TRIAD: THE EVOLUTION OF TREATMENT FOR CHEMICAL DEPENDENCY

by Cynthia Downing

This is an exciting new book that summarizes the three stage evolution of chemical dependency treatment. The first stage is the development of Alcoholics Anonymous (AA) and the 12-Step Tradition. The second stage is the development of the Minnesota Model and the treatment industry based upon its principles. AA and the Minnesota Models are a necessary foundation for the emergence of the third evolutionary stage— the CENAPS Bio-psycho-social Model. **TRIAD** presents this newly emerging model as an integration of past wisdom, current research, and an exciting vision of the future.

About the author:
Cynthia Downing, M.A., C.A.C.

Cynthia Downing holds a Master's Degree in Human Services from John Carroll University in Cleveland, Ohio, and is currently a doctoral candidate in Psychology at Saybrook Institute in San Francisco. Her dissertation research is on core issues of relapse. She is currently Clinical Director of Earthrise, a private practice specializing in chemical dependency and self-esteem. She has a special interest in long-term recovery and co-dependency issues. She is a Licensed Professional Counselor in the state of Ohio, a Certified Alcoholism Counselor, and a Certified Relapse Prevention Specialist. She is an author and lecturer on chemical dependency, and has made television appearances.

To Order, Call Toll-Free 1-800-767-8181

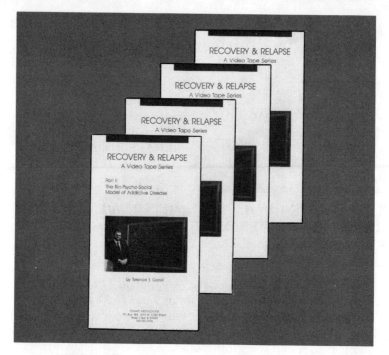

AN OVERVIEW OF RECOVERY AND RELAPSE

Videotape Series
by Terence T. Gorski

The CENAPS Corporation presents a four-step **video series** by Terence T. Gorski summarizing Addictive Disease, the Recovery and Relapse Process, and Occupational Relapse Prevention Planning.

Each tape is designed to stand alone, but when viewed as a series, a comprehensive overview of the recovery and relapse process is concisely communicated.

This series is designed for use in
- patient education programs
- staff training and development
- community education

THE BIO-PSYCHO-SOCIAL MODEL OF ADDICTIVE DISEASE

Addiction is a disease that affects a person physically, psychologically, and socially. This tape describes how the toxic effects of alcohol and drugs on the brain cause psychological and social problems to develop as a consequence of use.

The long-term aftereffects of chronic alcohol and drug poisoning (known as post-acute or protracted withdrawal) as well as methods for managing these symptoms are presented.

THE DEVELOPMENT MODEL OF RECOVERY

Recovering people need a practical "road map" to recovery, and this film provides it. Based on his clinical counseling and research, Mr. Gorski describes the recovery process as a progression through six concrete periods. Each period has a major goal and specific tasks required to meet each goal.

Failure to successfully complete any major recovery task can weaken the strength of the total recovery program. The result can be a cycle of low quality and painful sobriety called partial recovery.

THE RELAPSE PROCESS

Relapse begins long before a person ever begins using alcohol or drugs. Based on fifteen years of clinical and research experience with relapse-prone persons, Mr. Gorski explains the progression of warning signs that escalate from internal dysfunction, to external dysfunction, to sobriety-based loss of control, to chemical use. The general principles of managing these warning signs are explained.

OCCUPATIONAL RELAPSE PREVENTION PLANNING

Relapse is a major problem facing business and industry. It is only through the cooperation of employee assistance counselors and treatment centers that the problem of relapse can be effectively managed.

Mr. Gorski presents a five-step strategy for cooperation in the development of a recovery plan for the relapsing worker that can lower the risk of relapse in the workplace.

POST ACUTE WITHDRAWAL (PAW)
A Videotape Series
by Jan E. Black, Terence T. Gorski, and Daniel J. McEachern

Post Acute Withdrawal (PAW) is caused by the long-term aftereffects of chronic alcohol and drug poisoning on the brain. Many recovering people suffer from PAW and don't know it.

Terry Gorski, a nationally recognized expert on relapse prevention, and Jan Black, a counselor specializing in relapse prevention therapy, discuss the most recent methods for recognizing and managing PAW.

In these fast-paced presentations, recovering people discuss the techniques that they used to recognize and manage PAW. Aided by these personal experiences Terry Gorski and Jan Black summarize the most effective methods for helping individuals to recognize and manage these symptoms.

The presentations are powerful and informative. They need to be seen by all chemically dependent people, their families, and the professionals who treat them. The presentations are appropriate for use in patient and family education programs, staff training, and community awareness programs.

Preview Tapes

Keep these preview tapes for up to fourteen days. If you choose to place an order, the preview fee will be deducted from your bill. Postage and handling are free.

To Order, Call Toll-Free 1-800-767-8181

Lowering the Risk
A Self-Care Plan for Relapse Prevention

Based Upon the CENAPS Model of Treatment

by Merlene Miller and Terence T. Gorski

Lowering the Risk
by Merlene Miller and Terence T. Gorski

The choice to pursue a course of sobriety is the beginning of recovery, but abstinence is not recovery, only the beginning. It is essential for every recovering person to recognize the relationship between stress, post acute withdrawal, and relapse. This new booklet from the authors of *Staying Sober* presents a self-care recovery plan for long-term health management. Recovering persons can adapt the following ten steps to their individual needs: professional monitoring, self-help group involvement, daily inventories, reality-testing conversation, good nutrition, exercise, prompt problem solving, relaxation, spiritual development, and balanced living.

To Order, Call Toll-Free 1-800-767-8181

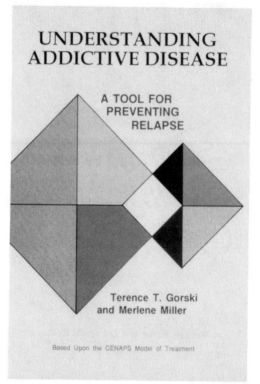

Understanding Addictive Disease
A Tool for Preventing Relapse
by Terence T. Gorski and Merlene Miller

Understanding the nature and characteristics of addictive disease can help addicted people avoid relapse. Many people fail to recover not for lack of trying but because of their limited understanding. Knowledge about the way addiction affects their physical bodies, their behavior, and their thought processes can provide a valuable tool for recovering persons. By replacing misinformation and mistaken beliefs with facts, people with addictive disease can avoid the destructive pattern of relapse and speed the process of recovery.

To Order, Call Toll-Free 1-800-767-8181

Foreword by Terence T. Gorski

Preventing Adolescent Relapse

A Guide for
Parents, Teachers
and Counselors

by
Tammy Bell

Based on the CENAPS Model of Treatment

Preventing Adolescent Relapse
A Guide for Parents, Teachers, and Counselors

Tammy Bell is recognized nationally as a leader in the field of adolescent relapse prevention.

This book is a breakthrough that is much needed. It integrates in a clear and easy-to-understand way the complex interactions between the symptoms of adolescent chemical addiction, the stages of normal adolescent development, and the presence of adolescent mental disorders in a number of clients. The ideas are sound and comprehensive enough for professionals while being easy enough for most parents to understand.

To Order, Call Toll-Free 1-800-767-8181

TRAINING IN RELAPSE PREVENTION

Relapse prevention planning is a skill that requires training, practice, and supervision. Most agencies are not equipped to effectively train or supervise staff in these methods. Since relapse prevention planning is such a specialty, CENAPS Corporation offers professional training through workshops and inservice training. CENAPS Corporation will also open a Center for Relapse Prevention within a treatment center or private practice. If an agency opens a Center for Relapse Prevention, CENAPS Corporation will train and supervise the staff, develop patient care protocols and patient record systems, and link these systems into an applied research network.

For information contact

The CENAPS Corporation
18650 Dixie Highway
Homewood, Illinois 60430
708-799-5000
FAX 708-799-5032